Killer Plants

Written by Kerrie Shanahan

Series Consultant: Linda Hoyt

T0359798

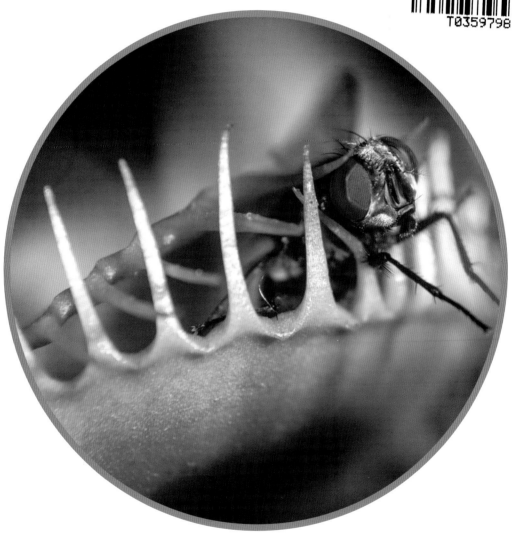

WorldWise
Content-based Learning

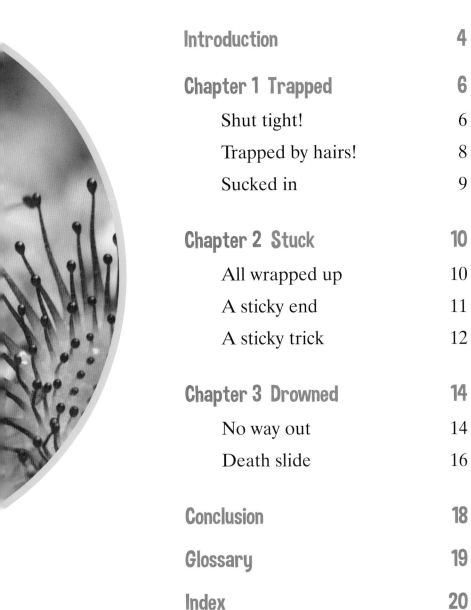

Contents

Introduction

We all know that lots of animals eat plants. But did you know that some plants eat animals? These plants are killer plants!

First of all the killer plants need to attract the insects, then they have different ways to kill the insects for food.

So you're probably thinking … *How do they do that?*

Chapter 1

Trapped

These killer plants trap insects to get the food they need.

Shut tight!

The leaves of this killer plant are a trap. Insects are attracted to the bright red colour of the leaves.

When an insect lands on a leaf, tiny hairs on the plant move. This tells the plant that something is there. The leaves close around the insect like a tight trap. There is no way out. The insect is trapped.

Venus flytrap

The leaves trap an insect.

Fun facts

☺ Some people grow these plants to get rid of unwanted insects.

☺ It can take the plant up to ten days to fully digest an insect.

Trapped by hairs!

This killer plant sets a hairy trap for insects.

It has no roots and floats just below the surface of the water in lakes and ponds. The leaves of the plant stick out like the spokes of a wheel, and at the end of each leaf is a trap covered with tiny hairs. When an insect disturbs the hairs, the trap snaps shut like jaws.

Waterwheel plant

Trap

Sucked in

It often grows in water. There are small balloons on each leaf. Each balloon has a **trapdoor**. When an insect swims past, small hairs on the plant move and a trapdoor opens.

The insect is sucked into a balloon, and the trapdoor shuts behind it.

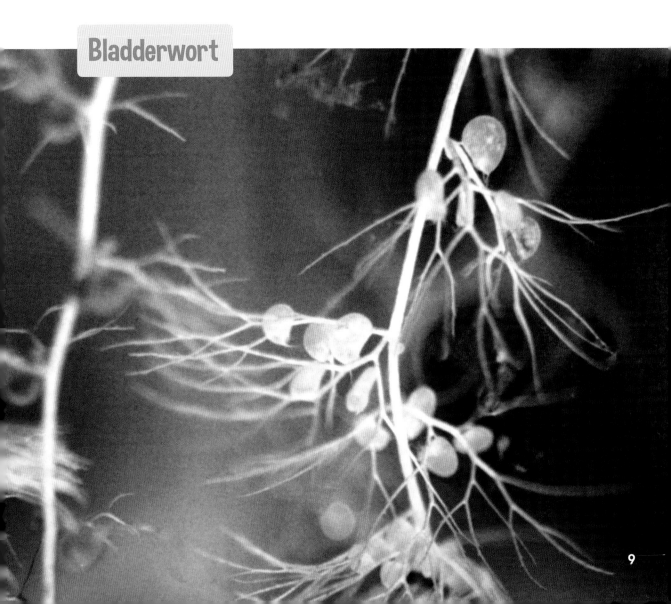

Bladderwort

Stuck

Some killer plants get the food they need by being sticky. When insects get too close to these plants, they stick to them. The insects cannot escape.

All wrapped up

This killer plant has long leaves that look like **tentacles**. The tentacles have sticky **nectar** on them. Insects are attracted to the nectar.

When insects land on the plant, they get stuck in the slimy nectar. The plant wraps its long tentacles around them. They are trapped.

Rainbow plant

A sticky end

Insects are attracted to the beautiful pink, white and purple flowers of this plant. When an insect lands on the plant, it gets stuck in a sticky **liquid** that covers the plant's leaves. The insect cannot escape.

This insect cannot escape the sticky leaves.

Butterwort

A sticky trick

Thirsty insects are tricked into trying to drink the drops on this killer plant. These drops look like water.

The leaves of the plant are covered with tiny red hairs. At the end of each hair is a drop of sticky liquid.

When an insect lands on the plant to drink a drop, it becomes stuck.

Sundew

There is a drop of sticky liquid at the end of each hair.

An insect drinks a drop.

The insect is stuck!

Drowned

Some killer plants use the **liquid** inside them to drown insects.

No way out

This killer plant is very big. It is so big that insects can get lost inside it. The plant has **nectar** that attracts insects. When an insect lands on the plant, it follows the trail of nectar.

The insect gets lost. As the insect tries to find its way out, it falls down inside the plant. There is no way out. The insect drowns in liquid that is at the bottom of the plant.

Cobra lily

Did you know?

This plant is called the cobra lily. It gets its name because it looks like a cobra.

Death slide

Insects slip and slide all the way down this killer plant.
Insects are attracted to the nectar at the top of the
leaves. The leaves are shaped like a **funnel**.

When an insect lands on the plant, it slides down the
steep sides of the leaves. The insect cannot get out of
the plant because the leaves have **slippery** hairs on them.

Pitcher plant

At the bottom of the plant is liquid. When the insect falls into this liquid, it drowns.

The insect is attracted to the nectar on a leaf.

The insect slides down the plant and drowns!

Find out more

Some large pitcher plants can catch and kill animals that are much bigger than insects! Find out which animals they can catch.

Conclusion

Most plants get the things they need to grow and survive from the soil that they grow in. But killer plants grow in places where the soil is not very good, so they need to feed on insects to survive.

Killer plants have amazing ways of getting the food they need. They have different ways to attract and trap animals to eat.

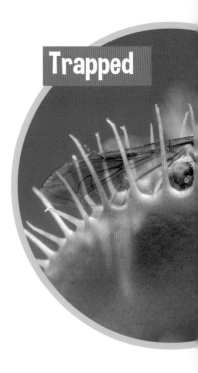

Trapped

Stuck

Drowned

Glossary

funnel a utensil shaped like a cone, with a narrow tube at the bottom

liquid a watery or runny substance

nectar a sweet liquid that plants make to attract insects and birds

slippery hard to grip

tentacles a long, thin, bendy part of an animal or plant

trapdoor a door that is hard to see

Index

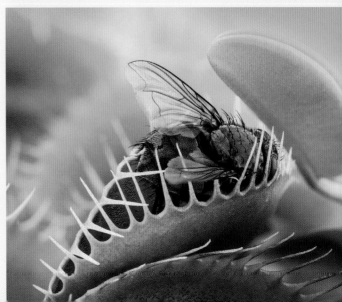